Resources for Dramatic Play

By Lois Brokering

Fearon Teacher Aids
Carthage, Illinois

Illustrated by Sally Cox

Entire contents copyright © 1989 by Fearon Teacher Aids, 1204 Buchanan
Street, P.O. Box 280, Carthage, Illinois 62321. However, the individual
purchaser may reproduce designated materials in this book for classroom and
individual use, but the purchase of this book does not entitle reproduction of
any part for an entire school, district, or system. Such use is strictly prohibited.

ISBN 0-8224-5811-X

Printed in the United States of America
1. 9 8 7 6 5 4 3

Contents

Introduction

Why should children be given opportunities for dramatic play?

Most children naturally involve themselves in dramatic play.

When left to their own devices, most children do what educators label dramatic play. I remember placing a hollyhock bud onto an upside-down blossom to make a lady in a full skirt. This lady then attended a party with other flower people. I also remember making leaf dollies, whose lives were remarkably similar to my own. My best friend and I worked for days preparing a "tea party" for our mothers in the attic. We were so disappointed when the mothers, enjoying themselves thoroughly, talked real "lady talk" instead of pretending they were our dolls' grandmothers who had come to pay a visit. I remember my own two-year-old talking to his pretend lion the minute I left his room at night. "Lion, where ah you?" "Obah, heah," it answered in a rather deeper voice! A two-year-old who came to see me recently played out a continuous stream of scenarios with a dish of pennies and a round crocheted circle someone had given the cat to sleep on. She chattered seriously to herself while her mother and I drank tea beside her.

Learning is accomplished through play.

Why is such a natural activity as dramatic play so important that it is included in nursery schools and day care programs all around the world? For young children, play and learning are not separate. Play is learning. Learning is accomplished as children experience, accommodate that experience, and then assimilate it. For learning to be significant, however, the play must be spontaneous and unstructured, rather than adult-directed and structured. Play is the basis for all the higher forms of mental activity that children will do later in life.

Play includes testing ideas and abstracting information from experience. This process may require repeating a play activity over and over or doing it in many different forms. Adults call this "practice." Through practice, children develop a feeling of competence as they master skills and better understand and control the world. Feelings of competence and of control or power build self-esteem. Unstructured play can satisfy children's needs for power over their small worlds.

Dramatic play develops social skills.

Through dramatic play children put themselves in the place of others. Young children, just emerging from the egocentricity of babyhood, need many experiences to develop social skills. Dramatic play allows children to be drivers, passengers, traffic cops, pedestrians, mothers, or big sisters. Children can better understand the correlation between feelings and behavior (and the consequences of behavior) by the use of dramatization. At the same time, dramatic play allows children to hone communication skills. Toddlers are content to watch other children play and to play beside them. Preschoolers begin to want to interact. "How is that done?" they wonder unconsciously. Dramatic play enables young children to discover the answer.

Dramatic play prepares children for symbolic thinking.
A requisite for adult abstract thinking and symbolic functioning (reading, writing, and arithmetic) is the ability to represent thought symbolically. Young children are seldom ready physically (even if they are ready mentally) to execute symbolic representations: written words. They are ready, however, to symbolically represent concepts, ideas, and feelings through dramatic play, movement, and artwork. The block corner, the art area, and the home or housekeeping corner are the parts of the preschool environment where children have the greatest opportunities to represent how and what they think and feel.

Dramatic play encourages visualization.
Before they can learn to read, children must have the ability to visualize. Visualization makes it possible to connect the real world of objects and experiences with symbols (such as those you are reading at the moment). For example, to understand the word *play* it must be possible to imagine or think about the experience of playing. People who cannot bridge the gap between reality and its symbolic representation through visualization have trouble learning to read.

Dramatic play encourages the use of imagination.
Besides developing cognitive and creative thinking skills, imagining allows children to be content without much stimulation from the environment. It has been recently discovered that being able to imagine helps children sit still and wait and even enables prisoners of war to endure deprivation over an extended period of time. When my young friend sat quietly on the couch with no toys but a dishful of pennies and a crocheted cap-napper, she had no problem keeping herself busy while her mother and I visited. Her incredible ability to make up one story after another, using pennies to represent children on an outing or at a picnic, made the time pass quickly and enjoyably without feelings of deprivation.

Dramatic play enhances problem-solving skills.
Spontaneous play enhances problem-solving skills. Children need to be able not only to solve problems, but also to discover them in the first place. Problems cannot be solved if they are not first recognized as problems. A rich environment in which to create play situations enables children to set up problems and discover solutions.

Children can release pent-up emotions through dramatic play.
As children play, they are able to release pent-up emotions or to prevent their submersion. In play, it is safe to act out fearful or anger-producing situations that might be forbidden in reality. In

play, it is safe to express reactions to the many directions, commands, and prohibitions inflicted on children during the day. Playing out these emotional situations enables children to gain mastery over them. By establishing a base on which to test emotions, children feel safe.

Children develop a sense of competence and control over their world through dramatic play.

In play, children are able to restructure and transform a world that often undermines their feelings of competence into a controllable, understandable world in which they feel competent. Children are able to assert their own feelings of power even over the seemingly all-powerful adults in their lives. Social competence begins to develop during the preschool years. Children move from parallel play where they talk to themselves and play alongside each other without interacting to social play where they dialogue and exchange ideas. Children learn how to make and keep friends. This sense of competence and control is a central part of building self-esteem.

Young children can develop many specific skills through dramatic play:

Intellectual Development
Problem sensing
Hypothesis testing
Logical problem solving
Creative problem solving
Attending to a task
Lengthening of attention span
Visualizing
Representing
Social/Emotional Development
Acceptable release of emotional tension
Taking another's point of view
Relating to another child
Exchanging ideas
Ability to entertain oneself
Physical Development
Large muscle
Small muscle

What is needed for effective dramatic play?

Children need space that is large and well-equipped with developmentally appropriate materials.

Both indoors and outdoors, young children need a place for pretending that will not interfere with other activities. A classroom I once observed had only a token dramatic play area to fulfill state requirements. Since only academic activities were valued, little space and no time were allotted for its use. The teacher then considered it a discipline problem when children used other materials in a manner she viewed as inappropriate—playing "train" with the sequencing blocks.

The space needs to be large enough to accommodate elaborate pretense and to be divided into two areas. One should be set up as a home. Since children spend most of their time in the home, most of their play centers around home themes. The second area should be flexible, because after a visit to a farm, a gas station, or an airport, children will have new ideas to play out. Props that suggest materials children observed on these outings will encourage realistic play.

The home area should have at least two sections: one for kitchen, living room, and family room activities, and another for bedroom activities. The materials should reflect the background of the children who will use them. If the children sleep on the floor at home or if their mothers cook with outdoor ovens, standard American nursery-school equipment is not appropriate. Most American homes contain TV sets, but how many preschools reflect this in their homemaking corners? What other materials are found in the children's homes? Food processors, microwave ovens, dishwashers, computers.

Dramatic play should be free and unstructured.

Children need not be asked to explain what they are doing or to structure their play according to a specific lesson plan. The suggestions in this book are just that: suggestions. Provide a wealth of stimulating materials and allow the children to create their own lesson plans and fulfill their own learning needs. Show positive support of the play by respecting the children's ideas and avoid evaluating their activities. In this free environment, dramatic play encourages creative potential and develops cognitive skills and concepts.

Simple materials that children can use to build, create, and imagine are necessary for effective dramatic play.

Provide materials that children can use to build what they need. Some examples are rug samples, ropes and tubes, pieces of fabric in a variety of textures and thicknesses, and boxes and boards that can turn into trains, planes, boats, tables and chairs in a restaurant, and beds in a hospital.

A box of throw-away materials (which should be kept in the art center) can provide unlimited props for dramatic play once the children realize the possibilities. Shells, evergreen cones, styrofoam meat and produce trays, coffee stirrers, popsicle sticks, corks, lids, caps, ribbons, bows, cardboard, small boxes, paper tubes from bathroom tissue and paper towels, plastic packing bubbles, wires, pipe cleaners, strings, yarn, masking tape, paste, glue—the list of possible materials is endless. Before depositing anything in the wastebasket, ask yourself if children could make play props by combining it with other materials.

Materials that have no label can represent whatever the children imagine. And you can help the children to see numerous possibilities even in materials with a designated use. For instance, an old leather purse can still be a purse, but it can also represent a suitcase, an attaché case, a mail pouch, or a grocery tote. Adults can both model and ask children to think about diverse uses of materials.

New experiences and materials should be introduced gradually to maintain a balance with the familiar.

As children develop during the preschool years, they move from purely sensorimotor play to symbolic play. In this process they move from the familiar to the unknown and back again. If new information is too different from what children already know, they are not able to assimilate it. However, if no new experiences and materials are presented, children become bored and are not stimulated to develop social skills, symbolic thinking, visualization, imagination, and problem sensing and solving skills. Determine how fast to move from the familiar to the unfamiliar and how much to present only after you have closely observed the children. By expecting and rewarding the symbolizing of experience, you will encourage maximum development of cognitive and affective processes through dramatic play.

When is the best time to provide dramatic play opportunities?

Provide dramatic play materials as a follow-up to a real-life experience.

Because children live in homes, role playing of home situations is universally appropriate in the preschool. Gear the presentation of additional materials to the children's experiences. Children who spend six to nine hours per day in the preschool will need to be provided with experiences through field trips and visitors who bring objects for the children's viewing. Budgets limit the number of bus trips that centers can provide, but walking trips and visitors can expose the children to a variety of subjects. A police car, with its two-way radio, screen, siren, and other special equipment, may contain enough stimulus to encourage many future play experiences. Confer with the police beforehand to establish the tone and purpose of the visit. You can use the experience to promote the idea that police officers are cooperative, helpful, and caring and to counteract the TV image of police work. Writing a group story after the visit about how police help us will reinforce these concepts and stimulate positive play.

Capitalize on serendipitous happenings.

If boxes of props are available in the closet or storage room, the visit of the plumber to fix a leaky faucet or any other serendipitous happening can stimulate dramatic play. Children will especially play out emotionally charged situations that they have observed, such as fire fighters putting out a fire. The wise teacher will react immediately by encouraging, rather than ignoring or discouraging the children's development of play themes.

What types of experiences should you offer to stimulate dramatic play?

Only choose from what is available.

Walking to a shopping mall may be out of the question, but perhaps a cow pasture is just down the road. Or just the opposite may be true! Planning according to what is in your own backyard makes sense because these are the things the children see, wonder about, and need to get to know more about.

Consider what children are able to understand. Taking three-year-olds through a plant where TV sets are made may seem to make sense because the factory is in the neighborhood and because the children watch a lot of TV. But if you take a dry run through the plant, you may find that the children will be unable to grasp the complexities of producing TV sets. Sometimes even an understandable process is made complicated by the way the company stages a tour. Children need to see a product manufactured sequentially. A tour through a bread bakery I once took with second graders proved to be a disaster.

The tour leader showed the bread being wrapped, then the room where it rises, then the mixing, then the baking, then the flour storage. The children had no way of comprehending how it all fit together.

Don't overlook simple, everyday experiences.

You can never take for granted that children have already had an experience. They may never have clearly perceived a simple thing like scrambling an egg. Stoves are seldom at children's eye level, and eggs are often scrambled when parents haven't time to pull up a chair, watch for the safety of children, or encourage the kind of "help" youngsters are able to give. Therefore, don't assume that all children understand and can play out everyday experiences. It is important for teachers to arrange experiences for children. And it is equally important to be sure that the experiences are understandable to the children.

What role should the teacher play in the children's dramatic play?

The teacher introduces dramatic play to the children.

Sometimes setting up a dramatic play area, complete with props the children have observed or used on an outing, is sufficient for a group to get started. At other times, you will need to introduce the new area with a tour and an explanation. You can do this at group time, with individual children, or with very small groups. You may choose to begin the play yourself. An astute teacher knows how to begin the pretending and when to gracefully withdraw: "Well, where are my car keys? I have to go to work" or "My baby is waking up from her nap now, so I'd better go over to my house" or "Well, thank you very much. I really enjoyed my pizza. You have a good restaurant here. Bye now!" These kinds of comments will allow you to remove yourself from the play without breaking it up.

The teacher is an observer.

Watch young children at play to determine where gaps in their knowledge lie and then arrange to fill those gaps. Movies, film-strips, slides, and books can expand and enrich the learning that occurred on a field trip or a planned experience in the classroom. Observing and asking questions helps you to discover what the children do not know—and then to search out materials or plan further structured activities to clarify the roles the children are attempting to play out.

When the play is breaking down the teacher should intervene in a way that gives the activity a lift.

Sometimes bringing a new prop to the situation will stimulate the play. "Knock, knock. Good morning, Madam. Here is the birthday cake you ordered. I hope you have a nice party. Bye now." Or "The train is full! Everyone who isn't already on may wait over here in the waiting room for the next train. Here are some old maga-zines to read until the train comes back." Providing materials beyond those normally in the dramatic play area triggers, rein-forces, helps elaborate upon, and sustains role play. A small item such as a hat or a paper punch may be all that it takes to encour-age a child to become the clerk at the store, the lady on a shop-ping trip, or the ticket puncher at the train station. It is important to be ever watchful for opportunities to help the children elaborate upon their play with small suggestions or additional materials.

The teacher needs to be authoritative and knowledgeable about what is being dramatized.

You may first need to become educated by visiting or reading about the theater, the turkey farm, or the bus depot. You cannot make suggestions or provide props without some knowledge of the dramatic theme being presented. Intricate details will confuse the children, but incorrect information is much worse.

What props should be used, and how can they best be stored and organized?

Sources for dramatic play resource kits or prop boxes include parents, Scout troops, service clubs, business people, government agencies, rummage sales, and garage sales. By posting lists of topics and related materials, preschools can encourage others to help assemble needed materials for the kits.

Divide your list into three sections: materials that can be donated or found at secondhand sales, materials that can be made, and new things to be bought. The planning guide on page 64 will help you organize such a list.

Find a source for sturdy cartons with lids in which to store the materials—one topic to a box. Label each box in bold, clear lettering. On the inside of the lid list the contents, with room for additions. Also list other materials that are too big to go in the box or that ordinarily are in use in the room. Paste a sheet of paper with the following information onto the lid: how to prepare the dramatic play area, what activity to encourage, and how to motivate the children to do the activity.

Find a suitable storage place—one that children cannot access—for the assembled kits. If the kits are to be visible in the classroom, obtain identical boxes and paint them with the same color paint as the wall, or cover them in tiny-print Contact or wallpaper so that they are as unobtrusive as possible.

As dramatic play resources are developed, introduce the staff to the kit's contents and possibilities. Dramatic play resource kits can be put together a few at a time to go along with units planned for the near future. Besides enhancing unit themes, kits can be used for special needs such as the marriage of a teacher, an unexpected hospital visit by a child, or a fire in the building. Normally, only one kit will be used at a time.

Plan for the care and cleaning of the materials in each kit. Will the staff members take turns doing cleanup? Will the director be solely responsible? Or will a volunteer parents' committee lend a hand? Kits should always be returned to the shelf in clean, working condition. Worn-out or used-up items should be replaced before the needed repair is forgotten.

Put out the props whenever they are suggested by the children's play or conversations, or whenever the props can support field trips and other experiences children have. A variety of ideas for dramatic play resource kits are suggested in this book, but the themes for the prop boxes that you can create are limited only by your imagination and by the children's experience. Children can only play out what they can visualize, and visualization begins with experience.

Be alert for new themes that may interest the children. Take your cues from them, and continue to build additional resources, drawing from the community and from parents for assistance. And remember, if you enjoy the activities you create, the children will enjoy them too!

 # ✈ Airplane

PLAY PROPS

cutlery
dishes
envelopes
magazines
paper
pens
small pillows
suitcases*
trays

DRAMATIC SETTING

chairs
cockpit window*
counter for ticket agent
headsets
instrument panel*
microphone
plane seats*
steering wheel

COSTUMES

crew hats (page 65)
scarves
ties
vests
dress-up clothes

*PREPARATION

1. Use old purses and totebags for suitcases.
2. Use blue paper with sponge-painted clouds to design a cockpit window.
3. Check industrial surplus stores for knobs and dials to fasten to a box for an instrument panel. Obtain some information in reference books on planes on how an actual instrument panel looks.
4. Line up hollow blocks or chairs for passenger seats. Number the seats with masking tape or old calendar numbers under cellophane tape.

PLAY POSSIBILITIES

"Passengers" can:

get ready for a trip by packing suitcases, dress up in travel clothes, go to the airport, purchase tickets, sit in the waiting area, board the plane, or eat a meal on board.

"Agents" can:

sell tickets or assign seats.

"Flight attendants" can:

show passengers to their seats, serve drinks and meals, and give safety instructions.

The "ground crew" can:

load the plane with baggage, direct the plane to move, and unload the plane after it lands.

HINTS FOR THE TEACHER

• Children who have never flown in an airplane will still be interested in play that involves airplanes. However, they may have misconceptions about the size of an airplane. Go on a field trip to look at planes on the ground, see a ticket agent at work, and watch the ground crew loading and unloading planes. Children might even be allowed to enter a plane.

• Have a pilot or flight attendant visit the classroom for a talk.

OTHER IDEAS

When the plane "lands," show the children a movie or slides of land with topography or climate that is different from your own.

UNIT POSSIBILITIES

Air
Transportation
People Who Help Us

Barber Shop

PLAY PROPS

Hairstyling:
hairbrushes
combs
scissors*
blow-dryer

Shaving:
electric clippers (cut
  off cords)
plastic pan
empty razors
shaving cream
shaving brush
shaving soap and
  dish
washcloths
towels

DRAMATIC SETTING

telephone
appointment book and
  pencil
old magazines
mirrors
doll for shaving*
barber shop sign*
chairs
tables
cash register
play money

COSTUMES

barber coats*
plastic capes

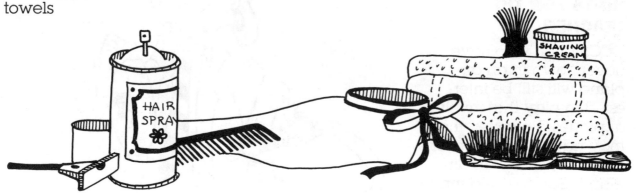

*PREPARATION

1. Make a doll for the children to use as they practice shaving. Stuff a pair of boy's pants and a shirt with rags or newspaper. Draw a simple face on a styrofoam wig holder and attach it to the top of the stuffed body. Attach gloves and shoes for hands and feet. Place the doll in one of the chairs. The doll can be a customer and will not mind being shaved repeatedly.
2. Provide materials such as cardboard, paint, crayons, or chalk for children to design a barber shop sign to post in the play center.
3. Use old white shirts for barber coats. Be sure to adjust the sleeves to a proper length for a small child.
4. Fold clear cellophane tape over the scissor blades so that they won't actually cut.

PLAY POSSIBILITIES

"Barbers" can:
dress up in the white-shirt barber coats, shave the doll (or other children), and "cut" and shampoo hair.

"Receptionists" can:
say, "Who is next in line, please?", make appointments, take payments, make change, and answer the phone.

"Customers" can:
wait in the waiting area or get a shampoo, haircut, or shave.

HINTS FOR THE TEACHER

▪ Help the children set up the area according to their own experiences. Perhaps they have seen a counter with a phone, cash register, appointment book, and so on.

▪ Check to see that the children are soap-free and dry before leaving the play area.

OTHER IDEAS

Set up the beauty shop and the barber shop side by side with the same waiting area and reception counter. Or, since both men and women frequent these shops today, combine the two themes.

UNIT POSSIBILITIES

Growth and Time
Changes

✂ Beauty Shop

PLAY PROPS

shampoo bottles
  (clean and empty)
towels
scissors*
combs
brushes
lotion bottles, powder
  cans, hairspray
  bottles, etc. (empty)
blow-dryers
nail polish bottles*

tray filled with hair accessories:
ponytail holders
clips
barrettes
curlers
hairnets

DRAMATIC SETTING

appointment book
  and pencil
old magazines
dishpan for basin
mirrors (both hand
  and wall)
dolls (for customers)
chairs
tables
countertop
telephone
cash register
play money

COSTUMES

plastic capes*

*PREPARATION

1. Fold clear cellophane tape over the blades of scissors so that they won't cut.
2. Fill empty nail polish bottles with colored water.
3. Use a large, plastic garbage bag to design a simple cape. Cut a hole in the center of the closed end for the child's head and cut two slits at the sides for arms.

PLAY POSSIBILITIES

"Customers" can:
wait for their appointments.

"Receptionists" can:
make appointments, answer the phone, take payments, and make change.

"Beauticians" can:
shampoo, "cut," and dry hair, or manicure nails.

HINTS FOR THE TEACHER

- Discuss experiences children have had at beauty parlors.
- Help the children set up the beauty parlor based on their experience and knowledge. Divide the play space into sections and set up chairs in each area: waiting room with magazines, sink area, haircutting area, manicure area.
- Be sure to respect the ethnic origins of your group. Additions such as hairpicks are crucial if they are used at home by children in the group.

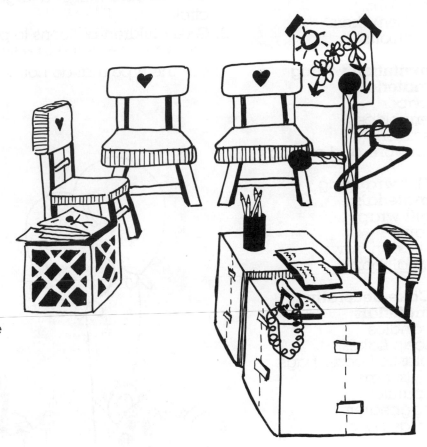

OTHER IDEAS

Set up the beauty shop and the barber shop side by side with the same waiting area and reception counter. Or, since both men and women frequent these shops today, combine the two themes.

UNIT POSSIBILITIES

Family
Me
Holiday and Celebrations

Birthday Celebration

PLAY PROPS

paper plates
cups
napkins
noisemakers*
balloons*

Invitation writing materials:

paper
envelopes
scissors
crayons and markers

Gift wrapping materials:

gift wrap
tape
stick-on bows
small boxes

Cake-decorating materials:

candles
soap flakes
plastic freezer bags
twist-ems
spatula
eggbeater
large spoon

DRAMATIC SETTING

"Happy Birthday to
  You" recording
birthday cake*
tables
chairs
dolls

COSTUMES

party hats

*PREPARATION

1. Provide a pretend undecorated birthday cake, using a cardboard box or a large styrofoam square or circle.
2. Give children balloons to play with that have already been inflated and be sure the noisemakers are the type that do not go in the mouth.

PLAY POSSIBILITIES

"Cake decorators" can:

mix water and soap flakes to the consistency of whipped cream and frost the cake. (Small amounts of frosting can be put into plastic bags. Close the top of each bag with a wire twist-em and snip off a corner to make a cake-decorating tube. Tint the frosting with vegetable coloring. Insert candles last.)

"Party hosts and hostesses" can:

set the table. (Demonstrate how a table should be set: fork and napkin at the left of the plate and the cup above at the right.) Hosts or hostesses can also greet guests, serve cake, and clean up when the party is over. They can decorate invitations with crayons or markers and deliver them to the guests.

"Party guests" can:

wrap small toys and boxes to give to the birthday child. (Provide a wrapping demonstration first.) They can sing birthday songs, "eat" cake, and thank the hosts or hostesses.

HINTS FOR THE TEACHER

- During clean up, wash the soap cake frosting off the cake to make it ready for another day.
- Remember that every child would like to be the "birthday child." Encourage children to take turns being guests, hosts, and birthday children.
- Combine this center with the post office play area when it comes time to deliver invitations.

OTHER IDEAS

Alternate theme parties with birthday parties if the children enjoy this pretense. For Valentine's Day or other holidays, the children can decorate the home center and make decorated cookies. Have the party at snack time and provide real food such as carrot sticks, crackers, or raisins.

Instead of frosting the cake, present a styrofoam cake that is frosted with plaster of paris. To give the plaster color, either add vegetable dye when mixing or use spray paint after it has hardened. Plastic candle holders can be inserted before the plaster is set. The children can decorate the cake with soap flakes.

UNIT POSSIBILITIES

Holidays
Good Manners
Friendship

Bus or Train

PLAY PROPS

hole punch
mailbags
old tickets*
stuffed animals
timetables

DRAMATIC SETTING

cash register
chairs or hollow blocks*
countertop
play money

COSTUMES

bow ties
briefcases
dress-up clothes
ticket agent hats
  (page 65)
vests

*PREPARATION

1. Obtain old tickets from a bus or train station. If they are unavailable, make your own with construction paper.
2. Have children help set up chairs or hollow blocks in rows with an aisle down the middle.

PLAY POSSIBILITIES

"Agents" can:

sell tickets, make change, and look up schedules in the timetables.

"Passengers" can:

buy tickets, wait for trains or buses, take a ride, and imagine what can be seen out the window as they travel.

"Conductors" can:

punch tickets and call out the stops at various towns.

Some children can be workers loading luggage, or putting mail or pets in the baggage area.

HINTS FOR THE TEACHER

▪ Since train travel is not as popular today as it was at one time, take the children on a field trip to either ride a train or see one. They may not even know what a train station or stop looks like!

▪ As children "ride along," encourage visualization. Ask children what they are passing by or what they are seeing along the way. Suggest certain items and encourage them to add other ideas. For example, "I see a barn with two cows in front of it" or "I see a whole field full of horses with a fence around it."

OTHER IDEAS

Large grocery cartons are ideal to use for the cars of a train. Add a dining car with some items from the restaurant play center. Simulate a sleeping car by using a few blankets from the house area. Use sound effects from a recording to enhance the children's play.

UNIT POSSIBILITIES

Transportation
People Who Help Us

Cars and Trucks

PLAY PROPS

computer cards
"careful driver" badges
safety seat belts*
dolls

DRAMATIC SETTING

stop-and-go signs*
traffic light (page 77)

Wheel toys:
tricycles
scooters
wagons
Irish mail

COSTUMES

police badges
whistles
shirts (color of the local
   police force)
police hats (page 65)

*PREPARATION

1. Make seat belts from plastic or jute chair webbing and buckles. Fasten seat belts to all wheel toys. Fix the wagon so that doll "children" may also be buckled in.
2. Make stop-and-go signs by mounting "stop" signs back to back with "go" signs on 1" dowels or curtain rods.

PLAY POSSIBILITIES

"Motorists" can:

drive vehicles and fasten seat belts for themselves or their "children."

"Police" can:

direct traffic with stop-and-go signs or the traffic light. They can issue traffic tickets (computer cards) for unsafe driving and "careful driver" badges for safe driving.

HINTS FOR THE TEACHER

▪ Help children decide where roads and intersections should be placed and mark them on the floor with tape. More help may be needed with this activity than with most dramatic play themes. However, encourage children to do their own problem solving by asking them questions rather than telling children the solutions.

▪ Provide opportunities for children to watch police in traffic control situations, meet police, or see a film or read books about traffic control.

▪ Explain the concept of taking turns involved with the stop-and-go procedure and be sure that children can interpret signs or traffic lights.

OTHER IDEAS

Set up the driving course outside. Use large blocks, cartons, and chalk or whitewash to designate the roads and intersections if sidewalks are unavailable. This theme might motivate volunteers to create concrete or black-top wheel-toy trails through the play yard.

UNIT POSSIBILITIES

People Who Help Us
Simple Machines

Doctors, Nurses, Hospital

PLAY PROPS

appointment book
clipboard and paper
baby scale
crutches
dolls and stuffed
  animals
flashlight
height chart on wall
wristwatch with
  second hand

Medical supplies:
Band-Aids
bandages
clean white rags
cotton balls
medical bag
"pills" in bottles*
plastic thermometer*
stethoscope
tongue depressors

DRAMATIC SETTING

cots
doll beds or boxes
blankets
sheets
pillows
table

COSTUMES

nurse hats (page 66)
white shirts or T-shirts*

*PREPARATION

1. Use small cereal bits for "pills."
2. A soda straw can be used for a thermometer.
3. To make a lab coat, use a white shirt and shorten the sleeve length. Attach red crosses to white T-shirts for nurse uniforms.

PLAY POSSIBILITIES

"Patients" or patients' parents (using dolls as the patients) can:
> wait in the waiting room to receive care.

"Doctors" and "nurses" can:
> give examinations or medication, bandage wounds, comfort, weigh and measure babies, and give medical advice.

HINTS FOR THE TEACHER

▪ Encourage young children, who are just beginning to take another person's point of view, to be sensitive to the distress of others who are hurting. Children can gain control over their fear of encounters with medical personnel through dramatic play centered around caring for others.

▪ Most children have had some experience with doctors and nurses, but they may not have had first-hand experience with hospitals. Decide whether the activity area will represent a hospital or a doctor's office.

▪ Be aware of sex stereotyping and encourage both boys and girls to try out all roles.

OTHER IDEAS

The school nurse's office or a local, government clinic frequented by the children is another possibility for input on the medical theme. If a number of children are having screenings or medical checkups prior to registering for kindergarten, dramatic play involving doctors, nurses, and hospitals will alleviate anxieties and answer questions.

UNIT POSSIBILITIES

People Who Help Us
Handicaps

Farm

PLAY PROPS

buckets
bags of animal feed*
seeds*
seed packets
baskets
plastic eggs and egg
 cartons
plastic vegetables
flowerpots
hay or straw

Tools:
rake
hoe
spade
trowel

DRAMATIC SETTING

tricycles
wagons
barn*
stuffed animals
table
chairs
countertop
cash register
play money

COSTUMES

overalls
farmer caps (page 65)
straw hats
work gloves

*PREPARATION

1. Obtain some empty animal feed bags and fill them with styrofoam bits, milk
   bottle tops, or large grains such as lima or pinto beans.
2. Use small pom-poms as seeds for the children to "plant" and cultivate.
3. To make a barn, cut a window and door from a large appliance box. Encourage children to give input and use original ideas as you construct the barn together. Use paint to put on the finishing touches. Or, use large blocks (cardboard or hollow) to create a barn in a corner of the room.

PLAY POSSIBILITIES

"Farmers" can:

plow the land, plant seeds, harvest vegetables, feed the stuffed animals, and wash the "tractor."

"Agri-business people" can:

sell the farmer's feed for the animals, repair the "tractor," sell gasoline and service the farm vehicles, and buy the produce.

HINTS FOR THE TEACHER

▪ Provide children with a trip to a farm or truck farm if possible.

▪ If you do not have a riding-size tractor available, create a toy tractor with a tricycle and wagon. Allow the children to decide how to construct the tractor and help them carry out the plan.

OTHER IDEAS

Set up the equipment outdoors. Designate one area, such as the sandbox, for seed planting. Set up the homemaking equipment in another area as the farmhouse. To support experiences the children have had, an apple orchard or chicken farm theme can be set up with a slight change of equipment. Substitute stuffed toy chickens for other animals, or apples for vegetables and eggs.

UNIT POSSIBILITIES

Food and Nutrition
People Who Help Us

Farmers' Market Stand

PLAY PROPS

paper bags
fruits and vegetables*
cider jugs*
plastic eggs and
   cartons

DRAMATIC SETTING

counter or tables
Farmers' Market sign*
"For Sale" signs*
cash register
play money

Wheel toys:
wagons
tricycles

COSTUMES

aprons (page 72)
farmer caps (page 65)

*PREPARATION

1. Provide materials such as glue, scissors, poster board, crayons and markers for children to design useful signs for the market. "For Sale" signs should include prices of various items as well.
2. Use plastic fruits and vegetables or soft sculpture or molded food items (page 73). Label cider jugs with apple pictures and the word "cider."

PLAY POSSIBILITES

"Farm family members" can:

wear aprons, take orders, put produce in bags, and make change.

"Customers" can:

decide on purchases and then pay for them.

HINTS FOR THE TEACHER

- After visiting an apple orchard, a farm, or a farmers' market where food from small farms is sold, help the children set up an area that represents the farm stand they have experienced.

- If they have seen a stand that focuses on one item (such as apples), include as many products made from that item as possible (Applets, cider, apple cookies, and apple pies).

OTHER IDEAS

Set up the play area in the gym or outdoors, so customers can drive up to the stand on tricycles. Farmers can also use wagons to make deliveries.

UNIT POSSIBILITIES

Fall
Farm

# Fast-Food Restaurant

PLAY PROPS

paper cups
napkins
small trays
paper bags
price list
burger and fries
  containers
waxed paper squares
  to wrap burgers
straws
waste basket

Food:

hamburgers and buns*
french fries (paper)
mustard/catsup
  dispensers
beverage pitcher
small milk cartons
  (empty)

Cooking utensils:

frying pan*
spatula
wire basket to "cook"
  fries

DRAMATIC SETTING

tables
chairs
restaurant sign*
cash register
play money
play stove
countertop
dolls and stuffed
  animals

COSTUMES

chef hats (page 66)
clerk hats (page 65)

*PREPARATION

1. Provide materials such as poster board, crayons, and markers for children to design a restaurant sign.
2. To make hamburgers, use cork coasters or circles cut from cork sheeting or use the procedure on page 73.
3. A grill or food warmer can be used in place of a frying pan. The idea is to provide the children with a place to "cook" the burgers.

1. HAMBURGERS
2. FRIES
3. HOT DOGS
4. DRINKS

PLAY POSSIBILITIES

"Customers" can:
use the price list, order food, eat and drink at the table, and put their waste in the basket.

"Chefs" can:
grill and wrap hamburgers, and cook fries.

"Clerks" can:
take orders, receive money, give change, dispense drinks, and give out burgers and fries.

HINTS FOR THE TEACHER

▪ After children have had a field trip to a fast-food restaurant or have initiated restaurant play, bring out the materials listed above and help the children set up the restaurant near the house area.

▪ Listen for vocabulary such as clerk, customer, order, price list and provide new words that the children don't know.

▪ Set up the waste disposal arrangement so that the paper goods can be reused.

OTHER IDEAS

Set up the restaurant outdoors. Provide wheel toys so that customers can drive up to the restaurant and give orders at the window. Then, children can pretend to eat in their vehicles.

UNIT POSSIBILITIES

Food and Nutrition
Taste and Smell

Fire Station

PLAY PROPS

old vacuum cleaner
hose with nozzle
ladder
hatchet*
map of city*
paper and pencils
bucket
sponges
telephone

DRAMATIC SETTING

fire engine*
countertop
tables

COSTUMES

slickers
red or yellow fire-
    fighter hats
black rubber boots

*PREPARATION

1. Line up chairs or blocks, or use boxes and cardboard
   to simulate a fire engine.
2. Use a toy hatchet or make one out of cardboard.
3. Prepare a large city map showing streets, intersections, houses, and other buildings.

PLAY POSSIBILITIES

"Fire fighters" can:

wear slickers, boots, and hats. They can ride the engine, make a siren noise, use the hose to put out a pretend fire, chop a hole in the roof with a hatchet to let out the smoke, return to the fire station, clean the fire truck, and, finally, hang up the hose to dry.

"Dispatchers" can:

take phone calls about fires. They can rescue cats from trees, or they might call the ambulance for injured people.

HINTS FOR THE TEACHER

▪ If children cannot go to the fire station, arrange to have the fire department bring a truck to school for a show-and-tell experience. This resource will prove to be helpful if a fire occurs in the building or somewhere nearby and the children need to play out their anxiety feelings about the experience.

▪ It is valuable for children to understand that fire fighters always clean up the fire-fighting equipment after a fire and get it in good order, ready for the next fire.

OTHER IDEAS

In warm weather, the children can use real water to play at putting out fires on the jungle gym outside. They can use an old car body for the fire truck.

UNIT POSSIBILITIES

People Who Help Us
Senses

Flower Shop or Show

PLAY PROPS

styrofoam or oasis*
flowers*
tissue paper (to wrap
  flowers)
cellophane tape
stapler
invoice pad
pencil
prize ribbons
delivery truck*

Variety of containers:
pots
vases
milk cartons (cut
  down)

DRAMATIC SETTING

flower shop sign*
work and display tables
countertop
shelves
cash register
play money

COSTUMES

smocks or aprons
(page 72)

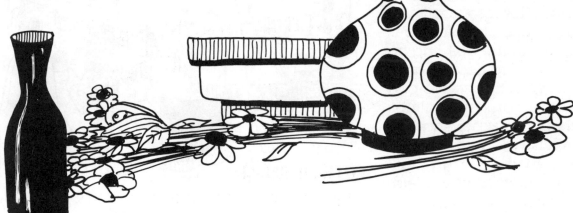

*PREPARATION

1. Oasis is the material florists use in the bottom of a container to hold the flower arrangement in place. It absorbs water well to keep flowers fresh. Styrofoam works fine for artificial arrangements.
2. Choose the type of flowers that are most convenient for you. You may choose to use paper flowers (page 74), plastic flowers, or real flowers.
3. Use an old leather dog collar to attach a wagon to a tricycle. This makes an excellent delivery truck!
4. Provide materials such as poster board, paint, brushes, and felt markers for children to design a flower shop sign.

PLAY POSSIBILITIES

Children can create flower arrangements and display them for a flower show. A group of children can be the committee awarding prizes while other children are visitors. Or, rather than having a committee, children might like voting for their favorite arrangements.

"Flower shop clerks" can:

design flower arrangements for display, write up orders, deliver arrangements, receive payments, and make change.

"Customers" can:

dress up in the home area and go out shopping for arrangements to decorate the home, pay for the arrangements at the flower shop, find a place to display the flowers attractively, and, finally, enjoy looking at and smelling them.

HINTS FOR THE TEACHER

■ Floral arrangements can be made to decorate tables in the room for a snack, a party, or a tea for mothers, especially if real flowers are available. Set up the props in conjunction with one of the following events:
a spring unit;
Mother's Day;
the wedding of a staff member;
a trip to a nursery;
an outing to a florist's shop or flower show;
a visit from a garden club member who gives a lesson in flower arranging.

OTHER IDEAS

If you are outdoors, additions can be made to include nursery stock, which can be delivered by "truck" (tricycle) or planted in the sandbox. Patrons can come to the "nursery on wheels." Include seeds and garden tools. Combine the Flower Shop or Show activity with a real planting project to brighten up the school yard or with a fund-raising bedding plant sale by parents.

UNIT POSSIBILITIES

Mother's Day
Spring
Easter

Gas Station

PLAY PROPS

bicycle pump*
"oil can" and funnel
spray bottle
paper towels
squeegee
old inner tubes
credit cards

Tools:
wrench
screwdriver
pliers
jack

DRAMATIC SETTING

gas pump*
cash register
play money
wheel toys

COSTUMES

shirts*
caps

*PREPARATION

1. If a bicycle pump is not available, use plastic fish tank tubing for an air pump.
2. Use a large grocery carton or appliance box for a gas pump. Attach a piece of discarded garden hose for a nozzle. Label the pump with the word "gas" and add some numbers for gallon amounts and prices.
3. Find or simulate shirts that have a gas company logo on the pockets or sleeves.

PLAY POSSIBILITIES

"Customers" can:

drive "cars" and "trucks" (wheel toys) up to the gas station and put gas and oil into their vehicles, clean the windshields, put air into the tires, and pay the attendant.

"Attendants" can:

help customers pump gas.

"Mechanics" can:

repair the cars or pump up an old inner tube.

Or, a child can be the person who delivers the gasoline to the station in a big truck and pumps it into the underground container.

HINTS FOR THE TEACHER

• Set up the gas station in the gym or outdoors where the children usually ride their wheel toys.

OTHER IDEAS

Set up the gas station outdoors and combine it with the car wash activity.

UNIT POSSIBILITIES

Transportation
People Who Help Us

Grocery Store

PLAY PROPS

toy shopping carts
fruits and vegetables*
plastic eggs and
  cartons
food boxes (empty)
cans
plastic bottles (empty)
paper and pencils
paper bags

DRAMATIC SETTING

shelves
countertop
cash register
play money
price signs*
grocery store sign*
wheel toys

COSTUMES

aprons (page 72)
shirts

*PREPARATION

1. Provide materials such as poster board, scissors, glue, crayons, and markers
   for children to design a grocery store sign and price signs for shelves and food
   items.
2. Use plastic, soft sculpture, or molded fruits and vegetables (page 73).

PLAY POSSIBILITIES

"Customers" can:
    make shopping lists, push shopping carts, and choose, pay for, and take home groceries.

"Clerks" can:
    stock shelves and help customers find what they need.

"Checkers" can:
    ring up sales, take money, and make change.

"Box boys or girls" can:
    carry groceries to the customer's car.

HINTS FOR THE TEACHER

▪ Most children will have had experience shopping for food. Help them to set up the store in a way that develops classification skills by categorizing food. Label the areas with pictures.

OTHER IDEAS

Set up the store outside or in the gym, and wheel toys can be used to drive to the store and take groceries home. Set up specialty stores to suit a particular unit or an available field trip, such as a fish shop or a bakery. Eliminate all other groceries in that case.

UNIT POSSIBILITIES

Food and Nutrition
Family

Housecleaning

PLAY PROPS

sponges
nylon scrub pads
dishcloths
feather duster
paper towels
spray bottles and cans*
dishpan
buckets
water
non-toxic cleaning
  solution

Floor cleaning supplies:
broom
sponge mop
dust mop
carpet sweeper
vacuum cleaner

DRAMATIC SETTING

Things to be cleaned:
chairs
doll dishes
mirrors
windows
easels
shelves
manipulatives

COSTUMES

plastic painting aprons
aprons (page 72)

*PREPARATION

Gather empty spray cleaner bottles for children to use.
Also fill empty spray bottles with water or non-toxic
cleaning solution.

PLAY POSSIBILITIES

"Family members" can:

take turns using the housecleaning equipment and tidying things up in the housekeeping area.

The "cleaning service" can:

pretend to clean an office or school.

Let children sweep or dry mop and then wet mop the bare floor. They can clean the rug or carpeting with the carpet sweeper or vacuum. Encourage them to dust shelves, scrub tables, wash windows, and so on.

HINTS FOR THE TEACHER

▪ Discuss cleaning needs with the staff and then decide what most needs to be cleaned and what will not be ruined by water or a cleaning solution.

▪ If the children have not experienced the materials by watching the janitor or a parent clean, help them understand how the tools work (for example, aiming spray at the dirty place) and how to remove dirt with friction and the help of a dirt solvent (soap or other solutions).

▪ Help children fill spray bottles, buckets, and dishpans with cleaning solutions or clear water. Cooperation and avoidance of sex-role stereotyping (for example, "Cleaning is women's work") should be encouraged.

OTHER IDEAS

As a first cleaning experience, take the children outdoors where the mismanagement of water is not such a problem. Add hoses to the rinse equipment. The jungle gym, outside walls, fence, storage locker, and other outdoor items can be scrubbed and later "painted" with water. A car-wash scenario is yet another possibility, preceded by a field trip to observe one in action.

UNIT POSSIBILITIES

Houses and Homes
Water
Contrasts

Library

PLAY PROPS

library cards
books and records*
check-out cards*
stamp pads
date stamps
pencils
box to hold cards
dolls

DRAMATIC SETTING

tables
chairs
check-out counter
record player
shelves for books

COSTUMES

dress-up clothes

*PREPARATION

Cut down envelopes to make pockets to attach to books and records as library pockets. Use scraps of paper to make check-out cards and to design library cards for students.

PLAY POSSIBILITIES

"Library patrons" can:

look at books, check out books, take them home to the housekeeping corner, and read them to other children or dolls.

"Librarians" can:

check out books or return books to the shelves.

HINTS FOR THE TEACHER

- After a visit to the library, help the children set up a play area that simulates what they have seen.
- Use the library play area in conjunction with a fund-raising book sale or the arrival of an order of new books.
- Inaugurate a system for children to take books home, or help those who are old enough to get their own library cards at the local public library.

OTHER IDEAS

If the children have experienced a puppet show or a story hour at a library, include puppets and a puppet theater, with pillows for a comfortable listening and storytelling area. Children can take turns reading or telling favorite stories to other children or to the dolls and stuffed animals.

UNIT POSSIBILITIES

Children's Literature
Fairy Tales

 # Parade

PLAY PROPS

rhythm band
 instruments*
batons
stuffed animals
dolls
flowers (page 74)

DRAMATIC SETTING

crepe paper streamers
record player
march music

Wheel toys:
wagons
tricycles

COSTUMES

animal hats (page 67)
newspaper or tissue paper
 hats (page 71)
band member hats
 (page 65)
tutus (page 71)
dress-up clothes

*PREPARATION

1. Make rhythm sticks by cutting dowels into 10" lengths and sanding the ends.
2. Put several spoonfuls of dried beans or rice into a L'eggs pantyhose egg, film container, or frozen juice container. Fasten the lid with a hot glue gun, or tape with plastic tape.
3. Sew jingle bells to elastic rings cut from tops of pantyhose.

PLAY POSSIBILITIES

"Parade participants" can:
be animals, band members, or performers in the parade.

"Audience members" can:
line the parade route with their "children" (stuffed animals) and cheer and clap for the performers.

"Float creators" can:
use paper flowers to decorate the wheel toys for the "float drivers." They can dress up stuffed animals or dolls to ride on the floats as well.

HINTS FOR THE TEACHER

▪ Children will be particularly interested in this type of play after seeing a real parade or watching one on TV. Provide such an opportunity if possible.

▪ Use this theme to teach the concept of lining up, forming lines by adding people on at the end, and staying in formation.

OTHER IDEAS

Children can have a parade for the dolls and stuffed animals, the 4th of July, New Year's Day, or some other special event. Set up a parade route and designate a starting and finishing point, where parade participants can assemble and dress. The parade can go around the inside of the building, the neighborhood outside, or the school yard. Hold a practice session in the classroom before the "real" parade.

UNIT POSSIBILITIES

Holidays and Celebrations

Pet Store

PLAY PROPS

books about pets and
  their care
collars
food and water dishes
leashes
pet food boxes (empty)
pet food*
pet toys

DRAMATIC SETTING

cages for animals and
  birds*
cash register
countertop
fish tanks
pets*
play money
tables

COSTUMES

dress-up clothes

*PREPARATION

1. Use real cages for pets or simulate cages by using cartons and screening.
2. Use real animals or stuffed toys for pets. Be sure to include a variety of pets, such as bugs and caterpillars.
3. Fill empty pet food boxes with small items such as shells, beans, or rice to simulate pet food.

PLAY POSSIBILITIES

"Customers" can:

buy pets and supplies, browse through books to learn what is needed for pet care, and make decisions about what pet is best for their needs.

"Clerks" can:

sell pets and supplies, feed pets, and clean out the cages.

HINTS FOR THE TEACHER

▪ Children and animals go naturally together, but being kind and gentle in caring for pets is quite difficult for young children. The lack of small muscle coordination or the inability to take another's point of view limits their capacity to understand and administer "TLC." Playing at buying, selling, and owning an animal gives children an opportunity for supervised practice with these concepts.

▪ Be careful not to show your own biases against certain creatures, such as spiders, mice, and reptiles. Teach children to respect all animals, not just the "nice," cute, and cuddly ones.

▪ Some animals, such as fire ants, scorpions, poisonous spiders, and poisonous snakes, merit respect for their danger. Teach children not to touch strange animals, even "nice" ones, All animals use biting as a natural defense when afraid, and most young children make the kinds of quick movements that frighten animals.

OTHER IDEAS

Some pet stores also groom animals. If children have experience with grooming, add a table with an attached leash, grooming combs, brushes, clippers (with tape over the cutting edges), ribbons and barrettes, and stuffed animals, including a large toy dog (preferably with long hair).

UNIT POSSIBILITIES

Houses and Homes
Animals
Reptiles and Amphibians

 # Picnic/ Camping

PLAY PROPS

Camping:
fish*
fishing poles*
compass
flashlight
food*
frying pan
spatula
logs or sticks
  ("campfire")

Picnic:
thermos*
napkins
picnic basket
plastic flatware
plastic plates and cups
suntan lotion bottle
  (empty)
logs or sticks
  ("campfire")

DRAMATIC SETTING

tent*
sleeping bags*
tablecloth spread on
  ground

COSTUMES

backpacks (page 75)
sun hats
sunglasses

*PREPARATION

1. Tie one end of a string to the end of a stick or wooden dowel and attach a magnet to the other end of the string to make a fishing pole. Make fish out of paper and attach paper clips to their mouths. The magnet will attract the paper clips and allow children to "catch" fish.
2. Use plastic food or make molded food shapes (page 73). Or use empty food boxes and containers and fill them with rice, beans, sand, or any other small items.
3. Be sure the thermos is unbreakable and does not have a glass liner.
4. Make a tent by covering a card table with a sheet or tie a sheet up by a rope from a tree outside.
5. If sleeping bags are unavailable, spread folded blankets on the ground.

PLAY POSSIBILITIES

"Picnickers" can:

pack up a picnic lunch and go to another part of the room or play yard to eat it. They may want to protect themselves from the sun with hats, sunglasses, and lotion.

"Campers" can:

wear backpacks and go hiking, set up a tent, go fishing, cook the fish, go to sleep in the sleeping bags inside the tent, and then pack up their things to take them home again.

HINTS FOR THE TEACHER

■ Whether the children play picnic or camping will depend on their experience. Provide a limited experience for children by going to another part of the property or a nearby park or yard for a picnic at snack or lunch time. Or, provide a mini all-day camping experience complete with sleeping bags (makeshift if necessary) at nap time. But don't expect the children to get much sleep!

■ Stress the importance of caring for the natural environment. Remind students not to leave trash on the ground, break or step on plants, or disturb animals. "Pack it in—pack it out," the motto of the U.S. Forest Service is a good one to teach children. Help them find all the things they brought into the area including any waste.

OTHER IDEAS

Invite grandparents or a senior citizens' group to picnic with the children. Or, hold the picnic on the grounds of a nursing home. Plan activities that all age groups can do together. Be sure the children are actively involved in the preparation for this play.

UNIT POSSIBILITIES

Summer
Nutrition
Family
Environment

Post Office

PLAY PROPS

boxes
brown wrapping
 paper
envelopes
ink stamp pad and
 rubber stamps*
mail pouch (page 76)
markers and crayons
paper
pens and pencils
picture of the President
scale
stamps*
unopened junk mail

DRAMATIC SETTING

cash register
mailbox*
play money
tables

COSTUMES

mail carrier hats (page 65)
mail clerk uniforms*
dress-up clothes

*PREPARATION

1. Make a mailbox from a grocery carton.
2. Use a blue shirt with the sleeves rolled up or shortened for a mail clerk's uniform. Draw a postal service logo or an American flag on the pocket with waterproof markers. You might be able to find an iron-on embroidery pattern of the flag.
3. Make rubber stamps by cutting shapes from foam insulation weather stripping with adhesive backing and sticking them to empty thread spools. Use the stamps on an ordinary ink pad.
4. Make use of old Christmas stickers or other promotional stickers that come in the mail by letting children use them as postage stamps on the envelopes they address.
5. Place the letter-writing and card-making materials on one table and the package-wrapping materials on a second table.

PLAY POSSIBILITIES

"Letter writers" can:

scribble, dictate, or copy what they want to say, put their letters into envelopes, address and add stamps to them, and place the envelopes in the mailbox. They can make greeting cards for special occasions, such as Mother's Day and birthdays, or for nursing-home residents.

Children can wrap packages and take them to the postal clerk. (Provide a package-wrapping demonstration beforehand.)

"Postal clerks" can:

weigh packages, stamp them with rubber stamps, sell stamps, and make change.

"Mail carriers" can:

deliver the letters from the box to the homemaking area or to individual children. (If children have symbols to identify their own cubbies, toothbushes, and so on, make these symbols available for addressing letters at the letter-writing table so that the mail carrier can deliver letters even if he or she can't yet read names.)

HINTS FOR THE TEACHER

▪ Involve children in writing thank-you letters to people who have hosted field trips, to persons who help at the school, or to class members who are sick at home or in the hospital.

▪ After some experience in writing letters as a group, take the children to a mailbox to mail their letters, or go to the post office to see what happens next.

OTHER IDEAS

On Valentine's Day, set up the letter-writing table with supplies for making valentines: red, white, and pink papers in a variety of shades and textures; scissors, paste, crayons, and markers; and heart stencils in several sizes (cut out of plastic coffee-can lids). According to the children's developmental level, either provide cut-out hearts or teach children how to fold paper in half and draw and cut their own hearts. Help each child make a mailbox from a paper bag or shoe box so he or she will have something for the valentines to be delivered into.

UNIT POSSIBILITIES

Valentines
Friendship
People Who Help Us

# Repair Shop

PLAY PROPS

tape (duct and
   masking)
scissors
Elmer's glue bottle
   (empty)
screwdrivers*
hammers*
wood scraps
dense sheets of
   styrofoam*
invoice pad
pencils

**Fill muffin tin com-
partments with:**
nails
screws
washers
bolts
nuts
cotter pins

Things to be repaired:
irons
hair dryers
electric eggbeaters
chairs
locks

DRAMATIC SETTING

workbench or table
countertop
shelves
cash register
play money

COSTUMES

work aprons with pockets
   to hold tools (page 72)
work belts to hold tools

*PREPARATION

1. Provide various sizes of hammers and screwdrivers and be sure that they
   match the sizes of the screws and nails.
2. Collect sheets of styrofoam used for insulation or packaging material from appliances or electronic equipment.

PLAY POSSIBILITIES

Children can pretend to be "managers" of the repair shop where broken appliances and other items are brought for repairs.

"Repair clerks" can:

use styrofoam and wood as "broken items" to hammer nails and screw screws into. They can write up invoices when the work is completed.

"Customers" can:

bring broken items into the shop, explain the problem to the clerk, and pay bills when they pick up repaired items.

Children can also pretend to be "family members" fixing broken items around the house.

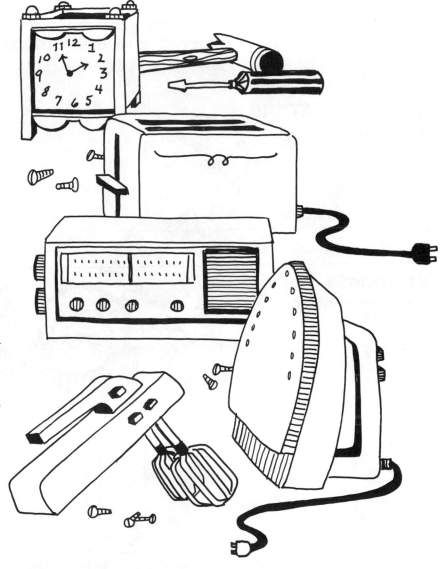

HINTS FOR THE TEACHER

▪ Use this dramatic play center to teach children that things do wear out and break with use. They can learn to bring broken items to your attention. Have a plan for removing these items and repairing them rather than leaving damaged or broken items in the room.

▪ Leaving broken items out for children to use models the concept that breaking and damaging is OK.

UNIT POSSIBILITIES

Houses and Homes
Machines and Tools

¶|¶ Restaurant

PLAY PROPS

dishes
cutlery
coffee pot
water pitcher
pots and pans
cooking utensils
food*
order pads
pencils

DRAMATIC SETTING

tables
tablecloths
chairs
cash register
play money
toy sink and stove
coat tree

COSTUMES

hats and coats for
  customers

Waiters:
white shirts
bow ties
vests

Waitresses:
aprons (page 72)
waitress hats (page 67)

Chefs:
chef hats (page 66)
aprons (page 72)

*PREPARATION

There are many options in providing "food" for the
children to use in their dramatic play. Plastic food
works well. If that is not available, make molded
food shapes (page 73). Or, use small items such as
seashells, pine cones, and bottle caps. Use real food
at times when the food will not spoil the children's
appetites for their next meal (for instance, at snack
time).

PLAY POSSIBILITIES

"Chefs" can:
   prepare food.

"Waiters" and "waitresses" can:
   take orders, serve food, and set and clear the table.

"Hosts" or "hostesses" can:
   seat customers, receive money, and make change.

"Customers" can:
   enjoy "eating" the food, practice using good manners, and pay the bill.

HINTS FOR THE TEACHER

▪Help children decide how the restaurant should be set up. Have children think about where customers should sit, where the exit and entrance should be, where customers should wait to be seated, where the bills should be paid, and where the kitchen should be.

OTHER IDEAS

Change the restaurant theme to a sidewalk cafe motif by setting it up outside. Extend the play by adding dishwashing as an additional activity. Set up the wash water, rinse water, draining rack, drying towel, and storage shelf or tray in a logical order. Provide direction cards above each prop to facilitate the learning of sequencing and following directions.

UNIT POSSIBILITIES

Food and Nutrition
Taste and Smell

# School

PLAY PROPS

alphabet cards
pencils
rulers
lined and unlined
  paper
crayons
readers and other
  books
dot-to-dot books
number games
flannel or magnetic
  board with letter and
  numbers
large clock
flag
dolls (to be students)

DRAMATIC SETTING

tables or desks
chairs
shelves

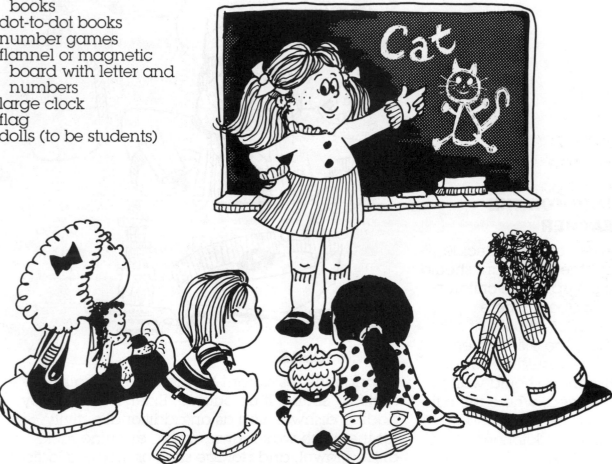

PREPARATION

Help children set up a school room similar to one they have seen or will attend
with tables or desks in rows. Place the flag prominently at the front of the area.
Place a container of pencils, a roll book, an apple, a phone, or a stack of work-
books on the teacher's desk.

PLAY POSSIBILITIES

"Teachers" can:

teach dolls, stuffed animals, or other children. They can direct activities, decide on tasks, lead a reading group, or assign writing projects.

"Students" can:

do writing projects, copy the alphabet, or do small number games.

HINTS FOR THE TEACHER

▪ Children about to enter first grade may have some ambivalent feelings of eager anticipation and uneasiness. Playing school can ease some of these fears as children work through their feelings and try out new activities.

OTHER IDEAS

Extend the play outside or in the gym so children can pretend to be physical education teachers and lead others in playing games. If possible, add balls and hoops to your equipment.

UNIT POSSIBILITIES

Changes

Use the school activity in the last possible week or month before the children begin first grade.

Shoe Store

PLAY PROPS

shoe boxes
shoehorns
paper and pencils
foot-measuring device
   (page 78)

Variety of shoes:
oxfords
sandals
tennis shoes
boots

For leather shoes:
colorless shoe polish
applicators
polishing cloths

For canvas shoes:
sponges
small brush
water dish
soap

DRAMATIC SETTING

chairs
foot rests*
shelves for shoe boxes
countertop
cash register
play money

COSTUMES

aprons for shoeshiners
   (page 72)

*PREPARATION

Use large hollow blocks for foot rests. Set them up in front of chairs for "customers" to put their feet on while trying on shoes or getting their shoes shined.

PLAY POSSIBILITIES

"Customers" can:
try on shoes and make purchases.

"Sales clerks" can:
show shoes, write and ring up sales, and make change.

"Shoeshiners" can:
scrub canvas shoes with soap and water or polish leather shoes.

HINTS FOR THE TEACHER

▪ Most children have had experience buying shoes, but not all of them may understand how to care for shoes. Take time to explain how to use a shoehorn, demonstrate how to polish leather shoes, and so on. Children need to learn to care for their possessions.

▪ Use the shoe size numbers to incorporate a math experience as well.

OTHER IDEAS

Any children who have experienced shoeshine stands on city streets might enjoy setting one up outdoors. Customers can drive up on wheel toys or walk up and have their shoes shined or cleaned. But, remember that children should not spend the rest of the day in wet canvas shoes.

UNIT POSSIBILITIES

Clothing and Fiber

 # Tea or Coffee Party

PLAY PROPS

napkins
telephone
food*

Clean-up supplies:
dishpan filled with
  water
dish drainer
paper towels
detergent bottle
  (empty)

Dishes:
teapot*
plates
cups
saucers
sugar bowl
cream pitcher
spoons

DRAMATIC SETTING

table
tablecloth
chairs
vase
flowers*

COSTUMES

dress-up clothes

*PREPARATION

1. Your choice between real food and pretend food will depend on how long the play goes on, how many children are involved, and what their attitudes are toward the need for food. The more realistic the props, the more involved the play may be.
2. If desired, fill the teapot with very weak tea or add a mixture of red, yellow, and blue food coloring to water to make a brown liquid. Add milk and sugar to the appropriate containers.
3. Make paper flowers to put in the vase as a table decoration (page 74). Dandelions also work well!

PLAY POSSIBILITIES

"Hosts" and "hostesses" can:

phone some friends and ask them to come to a party, set the table correctly or creatively, prepare the food in the kitchen, greet friends at the door, and serve the food graciously.

"Guests" can:

eat, drink, and be merry! They might also want to help wash, dry, and put away the dishes.

HINTS FOR THE TEACHER

• Orchestrate the consumption of real food so that it does not become the primary motivation for the dramatic play. Setting out real food just before lunch is not in the children's best interest and neither is allowing them to nibble all day long.

• These materials will be used more effectively in the homemaking corner rather than in a separate dramatic play area.

• The staff should be sure that children have clean cups to drink from. All dishes should be washed and sterilized an additional time by adults.

• If children are mature enough, include a small-group language activity focusing on tea party conversation.

OTHER IDEAS

This practice tea party is good preparation for hosting parents or guests from another school at a tea party. The guests can sit in small groups and be served by several children rather than the usual table arrangement that has guests line up for refreshments.

UNIT POSSIBILITIES

Food and Nutrition
Family
Good Manners

 # Theater

PLAY PROPS

programs*
tickets*

**Props for various
nursery rhymes:**
Little Miss Muffet
  spider (construc-
    tion paper)
  bowl
  spoon
  stool
Hickory Dickory Dock
  grandfather clock
    (page 76)
  toy mouse or mouse
    puppet (page 79)
Jack Be Nimble
  candleholder
  candle
Little Jack Horner
  pie pan
  crust and plum
    (page 79)
Mistress Mary
  watering can
  flower box
  pretty maids
    (page 80)

DRAMATIC SETTING

platform
chairs or carpet squares
posters of nursery rhymes
ticket booth*
cash register
play money

COSTUMES

Ushers:
boutonnieres
dark jackets

*PREPARATION

1. Real tickets are lots of fun to use, but small pieces of construction paper stamped with a rubber stamp (if you have one) will suffice.
2. Children can make programs by drawing pictures of the nursery rhymes to be dramatized or by cutting and pasting pictures from worn-out books or catalogs.

PLAY POSSIBILITIES

"Ushers" can:

pass out programs, seat the audience in the chairs or on carpet-square "seats."

"Stage hands" can:

set out the props on the stage.

"Actors" can:

act out the nursery rhymes, or narrators can say or read the rhymes while others do the acting.

"Audience members" can:

watch, listen, and clap when each rhyme is finished.

HINTS FOR THE TEACHER

▪ Provide children with the opportunity to observe a school play or experience a field trip to a real theater, if possible.

▪ As an alternative to using a platform, use hollow blocks covered with a rug to hold them together. Or, tape the blocks together with duct tape to stop them from separating and becoming a safety hazard.

▪ Use strings of Christmas tree lights as footlights to designate the stage area.

▪Protect the lights by placing a row of wooden blocks or a board next to them. Or, simply designate the stage area by placing masking tape on the floor.

▪ The audience can sit in rows of chairs in front of the stage or on the floor.

OTHER IDEAS

The play might evolve into a program for parents, for a Mother's Day tea, or for some other event. Set up a stage outdoors for a "summer theater." Half of the class can perform for the other half, or this might just remain a free-play option. The children can act out other scenarios besides nursery rhymes. Be prepared to provide additional props, or allow props from other centers to be moved to the stage area.

UNIT POSSIBILITIES

Children's Literature
Nursery Rhymes
The Arts

☞ PLANNING GUIDE

- First, decide which of the dramatic play themes fits your usual curriculum. For each one, organize your acquisition in the following categories:

New Things to Be Made
by staff
by volunteers
by hired worker
(carpenter, seamstress,
or other)

Used Things to Be Found
at garage or rummage
sales
at secondhand stores
at home
by staff
by parents
by service organizations

New Things to Be Bought
at discount stores
at drug stores
at grocery stores
at hardware stores
at other stores

- Plan a timeline for collecting materials, perhaps like this:

In two weeks we will have done the following:

In three months we will have done the following:

In six months we will have done the following:

In a year we will have done the following:

- Decide where you will store the completed resource kits. Select the types of containers you will use for storage and find out where they can be acquired (ice cream cone boxes, grapefruit boxes, paper boxes, purchased storage boxes, etc.)

BASIC VISOR HAT

(Use for band member, clerk, policeman, mail carrier, airline crew member, ticket agent, farmer, or train conductor.)

Figure A

Materials

    two 3" x 12" construction paper strips
    5" x 6" piece of construction paper for visor
    scissors
    glue

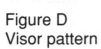

Figure B

Procedure

1. Staple the two 3" x 12" strips together to form a band to fit a child's head (Figure A).
2. Trace and cut out visor.
3. Cut on dotted lines to form tabs (Figure B).
4. Fold tabs up and glue inside headband (Figure C).
5. Decorate as desired to fit intended purpose.
6. For farmer cap, add a circle of net from an onion or orange sack to the top (Figure D).

Figure C

Figure D
Visor pattern

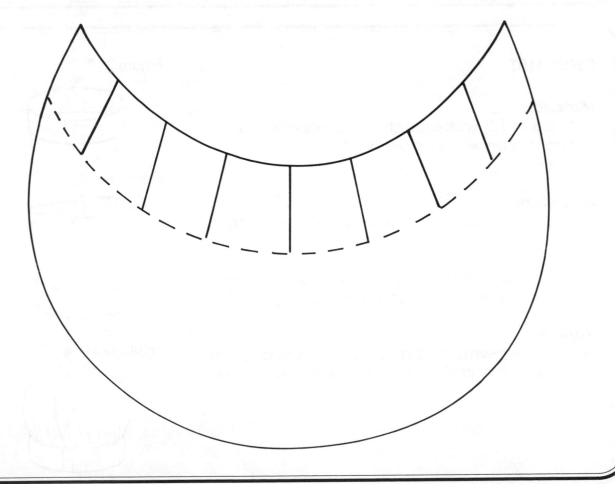

NURSE HAT

Materials
9" x 12" white construction paper or stiff white fabric
stapler
markers or crayons

Procedure
1. Fold 12" side up 2 1/2" (Figure A).
2. Turn the paper over and fold corners A and B down to C, overlapping them (Figure B).
3. Fold point D down 1 3/4". Staple in place but not through entire hat (Figure C).
4. Draw red or blue cross on front of hat. Fold over corner on front flap if desired (Figure D).

Figure A

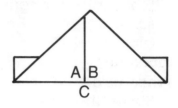

2 1/2"

Figure B

Figure C

Figure D

CHEF HAT

Materials
two 3" x 12" white construction paper strips
two square white paper napkins
stapler

Procedure
1. Staple the two 3" x 12" strips together to form a band to fit a child's head (Figure A).
2. Open up the two napkins and staple them inside the headband making small gathers (Figure B).
3. Gather the top together and staple (Figure C).

Variation:
For a more permanent and durable hat, use fabric stiffened with interfacing. Sew rather than staple.

Figure A

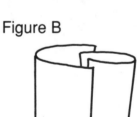

Figure B

Figure C

WAITRESS HAT

Figure A

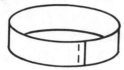

Materials

two 3" x 12" white construction paper strips
7" square construction paper (any color)
5" square white construction paper
14" fabric ruffle
stapler
glue

Figure B

Figure C

Procedure

1. Staple the two 3" x 12" strips together to form a band to fit a child's head (Figure A).
2. Fold the 7" square in a triangular shape and glue the ruffle between the two triangles around the two open edges (Figure B).
3. Fold the 5" square in a triangular shape and cut the two triangles apart. Glue one triangle on the front of the larger ruffled triangle (Figure C).
4. Glue the triangular design on to the headband (Figure D).

Figure D

ANIMAL HATS

Figure A

Materials

two 3" x 12" constuction paper strips
animal ear patterns (page 68)
construction paper (color and size to fit appropriate pattern)
glue
scissors

Figure B

Procedure

1. Staple the two 3" x 12" strips together to form a band to fit a child's head (Figure A).
2. Trace and cut out the appropriate animal ear pattern from construction paper.
3. Glue ears to headband (Figure B, C, or D).

Figure C

Variation:

Make animal hats from fabric using the cap (pages 69–70) and ear patterns.

Figure D

ANIMAL EARS Cut from construction paper. Or, cut from fabric and sew together. Leave bottom open and stuff. Sew to cap pleating front piece only.

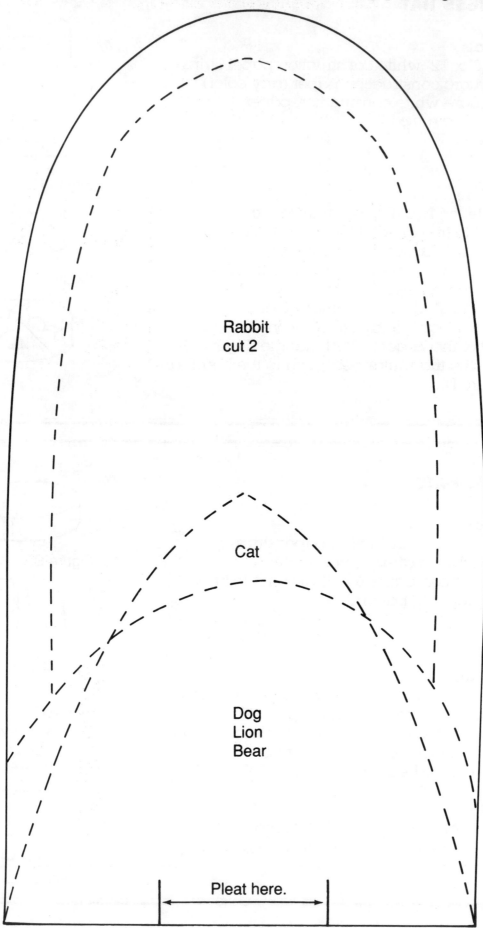

Rabbit
cut 2

Cat

Dog
Lion
Bear

Pleat here.

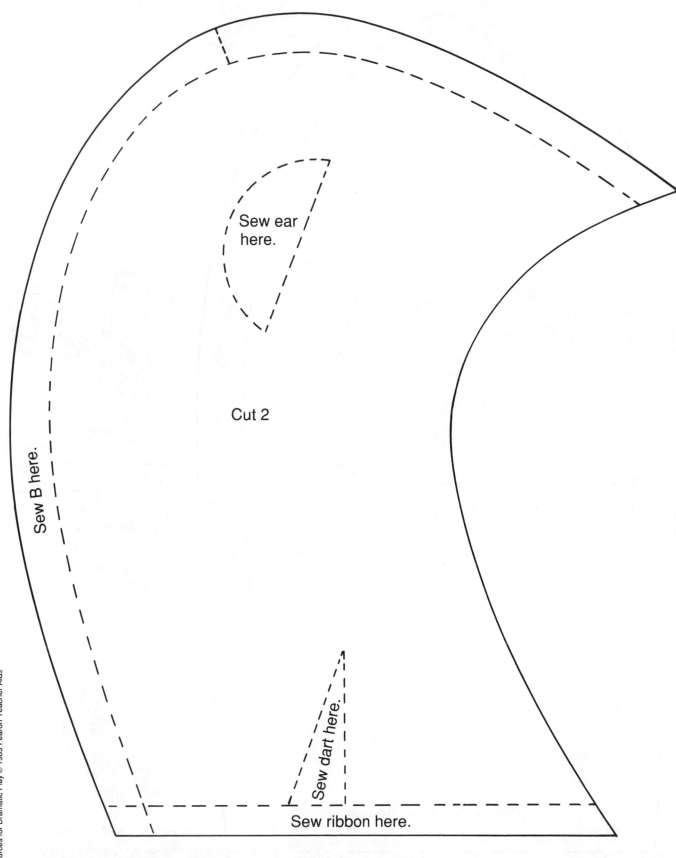

Sew ear here.

Cut 2

Sew B here.

Sew dart here.

Sew ribbon here.

ANIMAL CAP (BACK)

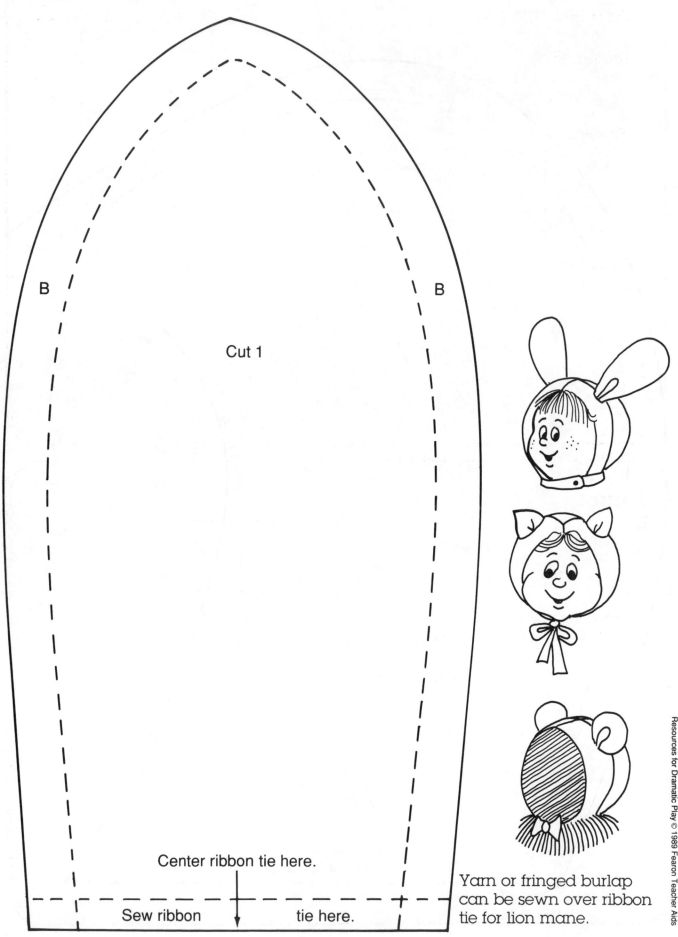

B   B

Cut 1

Center ribbon tie here.

Sew ribbon   tie here.

Yarn or fringed burlap
can be sewn over ribbon
tie for lion mane.

Resources for Dramatic Play © 1989 Fearon Teacher Aids

NEWSPAPER HAT

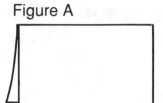

Figure A

Materials
half sheet of newspaper
crayons, paint, or markers (optional)

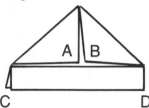

Figure B

Procedure
1. Fold newspaper in half (Figure A).
2. Fold corners A and B down to meet each other (Figure B).
3. Fold corners C and D up over each side (Figure C).

Variation:
After finishing step 3, open hat and flatten in other direction (Figure D). Fold corner C up to E, turn the hat over, and fold corner D up to E (Figure E).

Figure C

Figure D

Figure E

TUTU

Figure A

Materials
nylon net
elastic waistband from pantyhose

Procedure
1. Cut lengths of nylon net in 6", 8", and 10" widths.
2. Gather the pieces, using a loose basting stitch (Figure A).
3. Sew the 10" strip to the elastic waistband first. Sew the 8" on next and then the 6" on top to give a layered effect (Figure B).

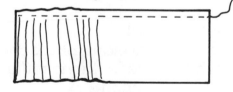

Figure B

BASIC APRON

(Adapt fabric and decorations or add pockets to suit intended purpose.)

Materials

18" x 20" piece of fabric
scissors
bias tape

Figure A

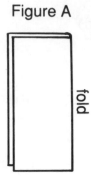

fold

Figure B

4 1/2"

6"

fold

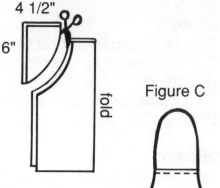

Figure C

Procedure

1. Fold fabric in half lengthwise (Figure A).
2. Make a rounded curve cut from the top to the unfolded edge (Figure B).
3. Open fabric and hem the top and bottom.
4. Sew bias tape around unhemmed edges making a neck strap and side ties (Figure C).

WAITRESS APRON

Materials

12" x 36" lightweight, black cotton fabric
38" white eyelet or fabric ruffle
42" piece of ribbon
scissors

Procedure

1. Round two corners of fabric to make a half circle (Figure A).
2. Sew the ruffle around the curved edge (Figure B).
3. Gather top edge so that it is 22" and sew 38" ribbon across top so that sides extend equally to form ties (Figure C).
4. Add pocket if desired.

Figure A

Figure B

Figure C

HAMBURGERS AND BUNS

Materials
socks (brown for hamburgers/white for buns)
scissors
needle and thread

Procedure
1. Cut off the toe from the sock (Figure A).
2. Stuff the sock into the cut-off toe section (Figure B).
3. Fold raw edge inside, shape, and slipstitch closed (Figure C).
4. Layer one brown between two white or tan circles (Figure D).

Figure A

Figure B

Figure C

Figure D

MOLDED FRUITS AND VEGETABLES

Materials
2 cups fine sawdust
1 cup dry wallpaper (wheat) paste
water
waxed paper

Procedure
1. Mix sawdust and powdered paste.
2. Add enough water to make a good modeling consistency—neither sticky nor crumbly.
3. Spread waxed paper for a working surface and shape dough into desired shapes.
4. Allow them to completely dry before painting with acrylic or tempera paint. Coat the painted pieces of food with polyurethane.

SOFT SCULPTURE FOOD ITEMS
Design food shapes using fabric stuffed with quilt batting or old nylons.
These soft sculptures are washable.

PAPER FLOWERS

petal pattern

Figure A

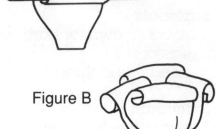

Materials
crepe or tissue paper
florist's tape
wire
pencil
scissors

Figure B

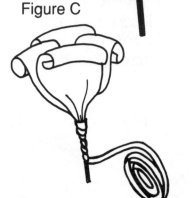

Procedure
1. Using the pattern, cut out 6–8 petals from crepe or tissue paper.
2. Roll the rounded edge of each petal around a pencil to curl it (Figure A).
3. Place petals with rolled edges to the outside around a wire stem (Figure B).
4. Squeeze the ends tightly together and wrap with florist's tape to secure (Figure C).

Figure C

FABRIC FLOWERS

Figure A

Figure B

Figure C

Materials
cotton fabric scraps
scissors
liquid starch
paint brushes
iron
wire stem
pom-pom

Procedure
1. Cut free-form flower shapes from cotton fabric (Figure A).
2. Poke a small hole in the center of each flower shape.
3. Allow children to use paint brushes to brush liquid starch on the flowers.
4. Iron the starch dry.
5. Insert a wire stem in each hole and bend it to stay in place (Figure B).
6. Glue a pom-pom or fabric circle in the center of each flower (Figure C).

BACKPACK

Materials
16" x 41" piece of denim fabric,
velcro, button, buckle, or snap

Procedure
1. Cut out pieces with the following dimensions:
   3" x 35"
   12" x 19"
   12" x 12 1/2"
   two 5" x 9"

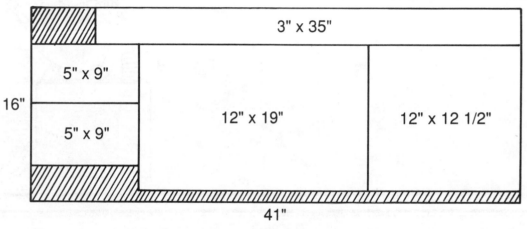

2. Stitch the pieces together following diagrams.

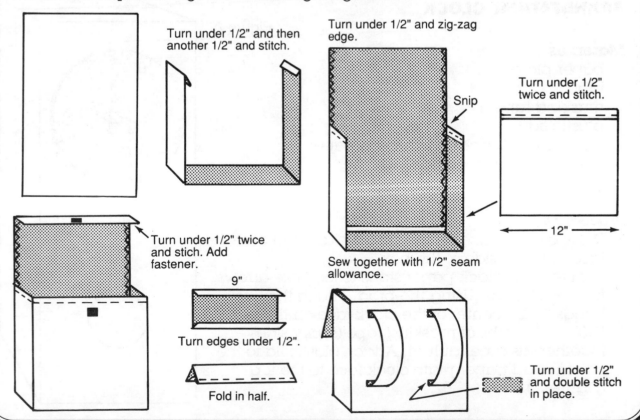

Turn under 1/2" and then another 1/2" and stitch.

Turn under 1/2" and zig-zag edge.

Snip

Turn under 1/2" twice and stitch.

Turn under 1/2" twice and stich. Add fastener.

9"

Turn edges under 1/2".

Fold in half.

Sew together with 1/2" seam allowance.

12"

Turn under 1/2" and double stitch in place.

MAIL POUCH

Materials
11" x 24" piece of heavy gray fabric
18" webbing or ribbon

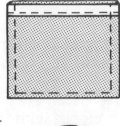
Figure A

Procedure
1. Cut fabric in half so you have two 11" x 12" pieces.
2. Turn down one 12" side of each piece and hem (1").
3. Place the right sides of both pieces of fabric together and sew around three edges (Figure A).
4. Turn right side out and attach the webbing or ribbon for a strap (Figure B).

Figure B

GRANDFATHER CLOCK

Figure A

Materials
paper plate
brad
masking tape
plastic lid
two strips of black construction paper
rectangular-shaped box
glue

Procedure
1. Draw a clock face on the paper plate and glue the face onto the side of the box.
2. Trim ends of black paper strips to look like arrows for clock hands. Using the brad, attach the two hands to the center of the clock face on the box.
3. Use two lengths of masking tape (sticky sides together) as a pendulum. Attach plastic lid to the bottom and paper plate clock face to the top (Figure A).

TRAFFIC LIGHT

Materials
半-gallon milk carton
black, yellow, red, and green construction paper
scissors
glue

Procedure
1. Cover the milk carton with black construction paper.
2. Cut three half circles from black construction paper 1" in diameter narrower than one side of the milk carton. Cut 6–8 slits, 1/2" long on the straight edge of each half circle (Figure A).
3. Curve the half circles and paste the tabs to the milk carton to form light shields (Figure B).
4. Cut out a red, green, and yellow circle for traffic lights.
5. Glue the lights just under the shields, covering the tabs (Figure C).

Figure A

Figure B

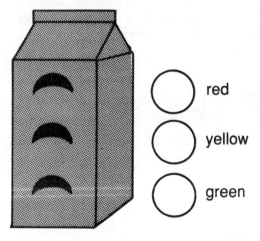

red

yellow

green

Figure C

Alternative:
Staple a red and a green paper plate back to back over a small broom. A child holding the broom handle indicates stop or go to others on wheel toys by turning the sign to red or green.

FOOT-MEASURING DEVICE

Materials

three 10" x 2 1/2" pieces of lightweight cardboard
10" x 2 1/2" piece of construction paper
tape
stapler
scissors

Procedure

1. Lay two of the cardboard pieces together and tape the ends shut (Figure A).
2. Fold the third piece of cardboard in half to make a crease and then open it.
3. Fold each end of the cardboard into the center to make four sections (Figure B).
4. Overlap two end sections and staple or tape together forming triangle (Figure C).
5. Place the triangle on the two pieces of taped cardboard. Slip the piece of construction paper loosely through the triangle and between the two pieces of cardboard (Figure D).
6. Tape or staple the construction paper to itself so that it holds the triangle in place but is loose enough to allow the triangle to slide along the cardboard pieces.
7. Draw lines and mark numbers on the flat cardboard to indicate shoe sizes (Figure E). Put the same numbers on stickers inside shoes.
8. Show children how to place a doll's or child's foot on the flat cardboard and gently slide the triangle to the toe (Figure F).

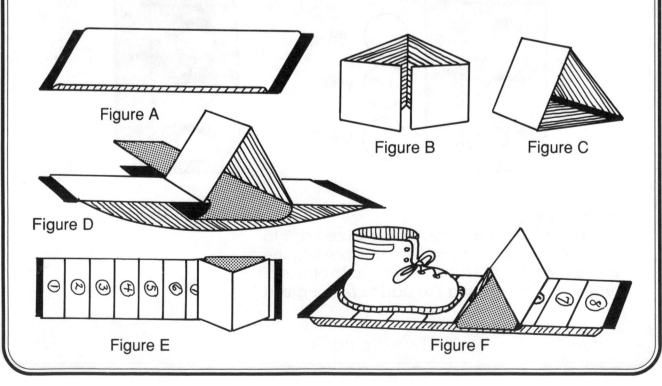

Figure A

Figure B

Figure C

Figure D

Figure E

Figure F

MOUSE PUPPET

Materials
- paper plate
- pink construction paper scraps
- small scrap of pink tissue paper
- black felt marker
- glue
- stapler

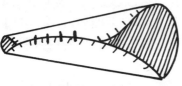

ear pattern

Procedure
1. Roll a paper plate and staple in place (Figure A).
2. Using ear pattern, cut two ears from pink construction paper and a 6" strip for a tail.
3. Staple tail in place.
4. Fold ears on dotted lines and glue tabs in place on paper plate.
5. Poke tissue paper scrap in the end of the plate to make a nose.
6. Draw eyes with felt marker (Figure B).

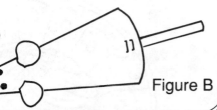

Figure A

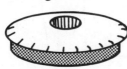

Figure B

LITTLE JACK HORNER'S PIE

Figure A

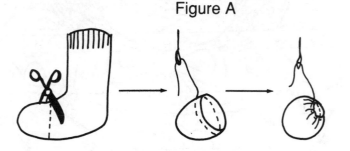

Materials
- pie pan
- old sock
- scissors
- needle and thread
- egg carton section
- tape
- heavy paper plate

Figure B

Procedure
1. Cut off the toe of an old sock. Fold cut edge into toe. Gather folded edge and pull up tight to form the "plum" (Figure A). Leave a small space for a child to insert his or her thumb.
2. Cut a hole big enough for the "plum" in the center of the paper plate. Tape the egg carton section over the hole on the top of the plate (Figure B).
3. Turn the plate upside down over the pie pan and fasten with hot glue or tape around the edges. Stick the plum into the hole (Figure C).

Figure C

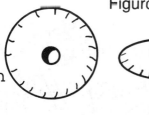

PRETTY MAID

Materials
- pretty maid pattern
- popsicle sticks
- glue
- flower box
- crayons or markers

Procedure
1. Reproduce several pretty maid patterns. Color and cut them out.
2. Glue the maids on popsicle sticks.
3. Arrange maids in flower box (Figure A).

Figure A

Resources for Dramatic Play © 1989 Fearon Teacher Aids